HOME AND SCHOOL STUDY GUIDE

THE NEW BOOK OF KNOWLEDGE

HOME AND SCHOOL STUDY GUIDE

THE NEW BOOK OF KNOWLEDGE

THE CHILDREN'S ENCYCLOPEDIA

A publication for

THE CHILD DEVELOPMENT PROGRAM

Grolier
INCORPORATED
New York

Dear Parents:

Your child is a unique individual in your unique family. This is why there can be no sure set of rules for raising him. How your child will develop depends partly on the self he inherited from both sides of his family, and partly on the experiences he has inside and outside his home.

You want your child to have the best that life can offer. You want him to enjoy life, to succeed in life, and to fulfill your dreams as well as his own. These are the desires of all parents.

When he is very young, you are his comforter. You heal his bruises. You praise each fumbling effort and encourage him after each childish defeat. You satisfy his curiosity. However, the day comes when his horizons widen. He discovers much that is new and strange and comes to you for information. Out of your learning and experience you try to answer his questions. Suddenly you realize how much more children have to learn today than when you went to school.

The fact is that recent years have seen an explosion of knowledge— amazing advances in science, prodigious progress in technology, and a rapid succession of world events. At the same time, a host of new words has been added to our vocabulary. *Laser, maser, quasar, bioluminescence, parapsychology, programed instruction,* and *language laboratory* are only a few of the new words coined in recent years. What can parents do to help children understand and master this bewildering array of new knowledge? What can parents do to help children keep up with the ever widening horizons of our world? The wise parent turns to books for help. THE NEW BOOK OF KNOWLEDGE, a comprehensive encyclopedia especially designed for children, is the logical choice.

An encyclopedia suitable for children contains the information children are likely to seek. It presents this information in language that children can read and understand. It is organized so that children can find information easily. The style of writing captures the interest and imagination of children and encourages further reading. And it includes a wealth of illustrations in full color—photographs, art work, maps, and diagrams to supplement and clarify the text. Your NEW BOOK OF KNOWLEDGE meets all of these criteria. It answers the questions that arise from your child's school studies because it is keyed to every area of the school curriculum—science, mathematics, language arts, history, geography, social studies, economics, anthropology, sociology, art, music, and health education.

The habit of turning to reference books for information is invaluable. But the close association of parent and child searching together for knowledge is even more valuable. Thus parents share with their child the experiences of his growing up.

Sometimes parents try to help children with their homework. In conference with your child's teacher you can discover her objectives for the class, and what the class is studying. Then if you take this HOME AND SCHOOL STUDY GUIDE and turn to the grade your child is in, you will find keys to the wealth of material in THE NEW BOOK OF KNOWLEDGE. The STUDY GUIDE will suggest many ways in which you can help him both in his school work and in the learning opportunities at home.

You can help your child, secure in the knowledge that school and home are working harmoniously together. With a gesture as easy as turning the pages of a book you can increase your child's opportunities and multiply his powers.

THE EDITORS
THE NEW BOOK OF KNOWLEDGE

To the Teacher:

We who have to do with children know that many facts we teach are soon forgotten. Not so the skills and concepts that we build, for these the child retains throughout his life if they are taught well.

One of the most useful of these skills is that of reference and research. You can teach the child where and how to look for information and help him form the habit of seeking it out and using it correctly. Once he has learned to use resources he can help himself toward any goal.

THE NEW BOOK OF KNOWLEDGE was planned and made by educators—classroom teachers as well as school administrators. The editor-in-chief was a teacher for ten years and a curriculum coordinator for six years. The senior editor in charge of social studies had similar experience; the indexer is a librarian, and many staff members are former teachers. The Advisory Board is made up of curriculum specialists in the various basic fields.

Beyond that, material was tested with children in the classroom before being published. Research in schools established the arrangement easiest for young searchers to use, and the pronunciation system that they could understand. Twenty-five school systems—in cities and towns and rural areas—co-operated in testing articles with children to determine reading level and understandability.

Reader motivation is built into THE NEW BOOK OF KNOWLEDGE. We don't say that THE NEW BOOK OF KNOWLEDGE makes teaching easy; we do say that it will make your teaching more effective.

THE EDITORS
THE NEW BOOK OF KNOWLEDGE

CONTENTS

Topics included in the HOME AND SCHOOL STUDY GUIDE were selected from the curricula of many schools throughout the United States and Canada. A great many additional topics will be found by referring to the index pages of THE NEW BOOK OF KNOWLEDGE.

Although grade levels are suggested in the HOME AND SCHOOL STUDY GUIDE, parents and teachers should also refer to related topics described for other grades.

All references to THE NEW BOOK OF KNOWLEDGE are given by letter volume and page, thus: A100 (Volume A, page 100).

HOME AND SCHOOL WORK TOGETHER

Parents are a child's first teachers. At no other time in life are growth and development as rapid as in the preschool years. It is sometimes hard to keep up with the changes that take place in a youngster from day to day. There are new words, new ideas, new interests, sudden changes in likes and dislikes. Learning is going on every waking moment.

Parents and the environment they provide influence the child's learning both in and out of school. More important than what a child learns is his attitude toward learning. Frequent successful experiences at home give him confidence to go on to new and more difficult tasks. Learning becomes an adventure—an enjoyable and challenging part of life.

▶ **SCHOOL IS A FRIENDLY PLACE**

Your child should look forward to school as an important and interesting part of his life. The attitudes that he has already formed be-

fore entering school can help or hinder that vital first adjustment to his school life. You, as a parent, can shape those attitudes. You can help your child to make the emotional adjustment between home and school.

References to school should be frequent, casual, happy ones. Your child needs opportunities to ask questions and generally feel right about this approaching adventure. He should look forward to meeting his teacher as a new adult in his life who will help and guide him. The teacher will be a friendly person who likes and understands children. Your child will come in contact with other adults at school too—the principal, other teachers, the school secretary, nurse, matron, custodian, traffic policeman, and the school bus driver. Your youngster should understand that all of these people will be helping him in one way or another.

Ideally, your child should have an opportunity to visit the school building before he begins school. Perhaps you can arrange to visit the school grounds before he starts. Walk around the building, look at the playground, and talk about what's inside. Assure him that his teachers and the other children will help him find his way—to his room, the bathroom, the place to get a drink of water, the lunchroom. These details are often the things that are most worrisome to a child.

Find out what the opening-day procedure is. Some schools ask parents to leave immediately; others feel it is better for them to stay part or all of the first morning. In any case, your child can be prepared for the fact that Mother may not be able to stay. This sometimes comes as a surprise to the child who has never really thought about it.

▶ SCHOOL IS AN INTERESTING PLACE

Your child will be working with all kinds of materials—paper, paint, crayons, clay, blocks, wood, tools. Some of these are already familiar to him, some new and strange but fun to try. He will find old favorites among the books in the classroom as well as many new and interesting ones. He'll hear music and learn new songs and games. There will be many things to talk about. There may be trips in the neighborhood, and plants and pets to care for. There will be times to work quietly, times to listen, and times to be active and even noisy. The wise teacher will take advantage of the child's natural desire to try many things. She will give every child the chance to achieve at his own level by providing jobs that he can complete satisfactorily.

▶ SCHOOL IS A PLACE FOR LEARNING

Your child wants to learn. He's eager to gain new skills and abilities, new knowledge and ideas. Schools recognize that children's natural interest and curiosity form a valuable basis for teaching. The model of the neighborhood they are building with blocks and toy cars in their classroom may lead to a visit to the shopping center. What children learn there is reinforced by reading, mathematics, writing, science, and social studies.

Besides the basic subjects that are uppermost in parents' minds when they think about school, there are other learnings too. All through elementary and even secondary school, children will be taught to communicate effectively through the use of pictures, speech, and written words. Early in kindergarten and first grade they will learn to plan their work and to carry out these plans. They will learn to work well with others and to be contributing members of a group. Every day they will gain in self-reliance, in the realization of their own capacities, and in their understanding of others.

▶ HOME-SCHOOL RELATIONSHIPS

Just as a child brings home the happenings of his school day, so he carries to school the things that are influencing him at home. No child can simply shut a door on one portion of his daily life and then take up another. For this reason, schools recognize the need for good home-school communication and mutual objectives. Many schools use parent-teacher conferences as a means of reporting progress. Others use conferences in combination with written reports. If your school does not provide time for regularly scheduled conferences, you should arrange to speak informally with your child's teacher. There are many things you can tell each other that will help both of you in working with your child.

▶ YOUR CHILD'S TEACHER

A teacher's greatest satisfaction comes from knowing that she has a part in a child's achievement. Teachers know that each child must progress at his own rate. Here is another place where parent-teacher conferences can play an important part. Find out exactly what the teacher is trying to do, how she is working with your child, her aims for the school year. Clear up misunderstandings before they have a chance to color your attitude, and your child's, toward school. Criticism of school can hardly help your child feel that school is important.

▶ WHAT ABOUT HOMEWORK?

Teachers recognize that some of the best learning often comes from direct experiences outside of school. There are many opportunities for learning at home. The five-year-old setting the table sees the necessity for simple counting. Fractions and measurements come alive for the youngster who helps his mother bake a cake. Helping your child write his own thank-you notes after his birthday and Christmas gives practice in writing and spelling. A visit to the supermarket or the place where Daddy works is an exercise in social studies. These are examples of homework in the best sense of the word.

Sometimes the best homework bears little relationship to the work being done at school, but serves to enrich the child's total living. Music or dancing lessons, a trip to the zoo or the museum, travel to another city, membership in a club—all of these are contributions to the child's education in the broadest sense.

Your child's own library of reference books, stories, and factual books are important too. Books keep alive a child's interest in reading for pleasure and information and help to build a foundation for developing the reading habit. The HOME AND SCHOOL READING GUIDE which accompanies your NEW BOOK OF KNOWLEDGE contains many valuable suggestions.

▶ HOME ENVIRONMENT AND THE TOOLS FOR LEARNING

We hear a lot about providing a child with an enriched environment—the kind that has nothing to do with money. This simply means purposely creating an environment in which children have the opportunity to develop and to learn. It isn't difficult to build this environment for your child when you remember what children need.

A child needs security—security which assures him that he is a real member of the family and has the loving support of his parents.

A child needs freedom—both physical and mental.

A child needs limits—thoughtfully and firmly established and consistently maintained.

A child needs help, not hovering overprotection; guidance, not interference; and just enough supervision for his protection.

A child needs honest praise and encouragement.

A child needs an example of good living.

A child needs a well-organized home.

A child needs a quiet corner where he can read a book or use the encyclopedia or other reference materials.

Tools for Learning

Given this kind of atmosphere to grow in, your child also needs the tools for learning.

A child needs music—opportunities to hear good music on radio, television, and the wonderful records produced for children today; experiences in creating music with simple instruments and later with real instruments; and by singing.

A child needs arts and crafts materials—clay, paint, paper, crayons, cloth, paste, wood, scissors, and other tools. All of these things become wonderful play materials for children.

A child needs books—all kinds of books to meet his different needs: realistic and fanciful stories; reference books for factual information; books to be shared by the whole family and books to be enjoyed by the child alone; picture books to look at and talk about.

Learning begins and continues at home. You can help your child to be eager to learn, to be enthusiastic about trying new things. You can encourage him to think for himself, to be creative and ready to explore. That is learning.

KINDERGARTEN AND GRADES 1–3

▶ MEET THE YOUNGER ELEMENTARY SCHOOL CHILD

Even though each child grows and learns at his own pace, nearly all children go through similar stages of development. Teachers in kindergarten and the early childhood grades recognize these growth characteristics. At the same time, they take into account the individual physical, emotional, and mental differences of early-grade children when they plan the school program for the younger elementary school child.

Teachers know that large muscles develop more rapidly than small muscles. Consequently, early graders need outdoor play—jumping, running, and climbing. While he jumps, runs, and climbs, your child learns a great deal about the world and the people around him, for children learn in many ways—with their eyes, ears, and bodies as well as with their minds.

Your child needs quiet times and rest periods, too, for he tires easily. His heart is growing rapidly, while his lungs are still relatively small. And so there are times for rest, for listening to songs and stories and poring through picture books, and for caring for plants and animals.

This is a time of transition. It hasn't been easy for your child to leave the warm comfort of being at home with Mother, even though school offers excitement and the glamour of growing up. Tears sometimes well up quickly. Tempers sometimes flare. Feelings can be hurt and possessions disputed. The young child has much to learn about himself and about getting along with others. He needs understanding and a chance to develop self-confidence.

Each early-grader develops according to his own growth rate. Some children may be full of action and speed, fidgety and restless, and eager to run or to throw a ball. Others, whose muscular control of smaller muscles is more advanced, may enjoy sewing, cutting, pasting, drawing, coloring, and writing. But all youngsters at this developmental level are quite concerned with large ideas—with the immensity of space and the universe, with the wonders of nature and of God.

This is a wonderful age, but it is a trying one for both the child and his parents, for the child is reaching out in his own way to a wide and exciting new world. The early-grader is still very young, and so very much is expected of him. He needs support, understanding, and friendship. And he needs to feel that you accept him and appreciate what he can do.

LANGUAGE ARTS

The language arts started in the crib, for that's where your child began to learn the many sounds he now uses in talking and listening. With his first lusty cries he began to realize that sound carries both meaning and feeling. Your response taught him that. As he grew, he gradually understood that spoken words are messengers that carry meaning from speaker to listener.

As you read to your child, he saw the printed words in the book. He couldn't read them, of course, but he did understand that written and printed words had meaning. In the primary grades he learns the magic of unlocking meaning from those printed symbols on a page.

Many things influence a child's language, but those nearest to him—you, his parents—have the greatest effect on his language growth. As he catches your attitudes, feelings, and thoughts, he realizes that what you say and how you say it tells others what you mean and how you mean it.

Where you live, your choice of words, your work, your personality, and many other factors influence family talk and your child's speech. As he uses words to express feelings and facts, questions and answers, he learns that we use language as we seek information. When you ask "What do you think?" he learns that children do not have a monopoly on questions, and that you care about his opinions. When he sees you look it up in THE NEW BOOK OF KNOWLEDGE he learns that although adults do not know all the answers, we do know where and how to find many of them.

In dozens of ways parents teach preschoolers the meaning and use of language. Once children go out into the neighborhood and to schools, other influences shape their language. Television, radio, and motion pictures introduce new words, new accents, and new uses of words to their sharp young ears and tongues. Books bring freshly minted phrases from a writer's rich imagination. The neighbor's child shares more than his toys, for he shares his language inheritance too. But of all the many influences that affect your child's language, yours is still the strongest. Consciously or not, you are still his most important teacher. You can help your child to select and edit his speech, to spark it and stretch for new ways of expressing ideas, facts, and feelings. You can help him develop discrimination in television viewing. And you can expose him early to the joys of reading.

▶ THE LANGUAGE ARTS IN KINDERGARTEN AND THE PRIMARY GRADES

Ours is a verbal society. How much a child learns both in and out of school depends largely on his ability to use and understand language. As he learns by watching and doing, he uses words to clarify his ideas. As he listens, talks with others, reads, and writes, the school child uses words as he thinks.

The language arts are used and taught throughout the school day. Of course, special periods are set aside for skill development in reading, writing, spelling, and composition, but language is used in social studies, science, mathematics, and in all other studies and activities in the classroom and on the playground.

The description of the language-arts curriculum that follows presents ways parents can tie home and school experiences together as they help their children learn to use our language well.

▶ SPEAKING

We express feelings and meaning through the tone, inflection, rhythm, and mood of our speech as well as through our words.

Poetry. Listening to poetry can help children hear the rhythm, the lilt, and the richness of our language. Rhyme not only delights children but alerts them to the similarity of sounds. If the ideas and the imagery are simple, poems can introduce youngsters to new words and help them expand their imaginations and their vocabularies.

Courtesy. If children are to communicate effectively, they must learn to use appropriate language and observe language courtesy. When you say "Please" and "Thank you," your child learns that consideration for others dictates good manners and that good manners can be expressed verbally.

Observation. Children learn to speak best when they have something they want to say. Help your child to enjoy the world around him. Teach him to observe and to talk about what he sees. Help him to engage in activities that he can discuss and describe. The youngster who is encouraged this way has something to share with others. Dozens of activities described in THE NEW BOOK OF KNOWLEDGE help children observe the natural wonders around them and engage in experimentation and construction. These experiences provide opportunities for developing new interests, understandings, and enthusiasms. Such interests are necessary for future reading and speaking success.

▶ **LISTENING**

This is truly an age of listening. Television, motion pictures, lectures, the theater, radio, and recordings have attuned our ears to the talk of others. All through school and life we must listen courteously and attentively when others speak.

The art of listening must be taught to children, and the kindergarten and primary grade teacher does this with plan and purpose. She knows that the child who sits at rigid attention with folded hands may be a million miles away from the words that are floating in his direction. She knows, too, that if she wishes to

catch his ear, she must capture his interest through purposeful teaching.

During kindergarten and the primary years your youngster will learn to listen to: a) simple rules and directions; b) answers to his many questions; c) stories and poems; d) recordings, the school public address system, radio, television, motion pictures, and filmstrips with sound.

Of course, you do these things at home too. Home is the place for varied and informal oral language. In dozens of ways parents encourage children to speak well and listen carefully. THE NEW BOOK OF KNOWLEDGE provides material for many and varied language-arts experiences. These include stories, poems, plays, games, selections for reading aloud, suggestions for listening experiences, games, riddles, puzzles, and many, many more.

SPEAKING AND LISTENING

▶ **HOW YOUR CHILD'S TEACHER HELPS**

Your child's teacher will try to create a comfortable, receptive, and lively classroom atmosphere so that children will talk easily and well. The teacher will guide your child by helping him to organize and edit his thoughts. She will help him develop a sense of idea sequence and show him how to stick to a point in his conversation. Using various tools and techniques, she will teach spoken language skills as they are used in conversation, discussion, planning, reporting, interviewing, telephoning, delivering messages, extending invitations and thank you's, making announcements, storytelling, oral reading, reciting poetry, and dramatic play.

Your child's teacher sets aside special times each day when she encourages the class to share special experiences. And so your child learns to stand on his feet and communicate with ease and charm. The modern classroom is a place of continuously shared experiences and ideas, for as children learn, they engage in the easy exchange of ideas carried on through talk.

▶ READING AND LITERATURE

The reading program that begins in the primary grades has two objectives—the perfection of the mechanics of reading, and the development of lifetime reading habits.

In the primary grades your child will learn to read and understand simple signs, charts, and books. He will learn that certain groups of letters have particular sounds. He'll learn that words often take their meanings from other words in the sentence, and he'll learn how to judge what he reads. He'll read for feeling and for fun as well as for information, ideas, and facts.

You can help your child at home, too. When you look at pictures together you can help him gather meanings, discern differences, and group similar ideas. He may describe what he sees as he learns to cope with a picture's meaning, and he will grasp differences. This is important preparation for learning to read in school, because he will have to recognize differences in word length and word shape. He'll have to learn to organize and interpret what he reads. Pictures help children link their visual experiences with the printed page. Photographs capture reality; drawings create mood. Both can provide additional information to supplement the printed page, and both are important. THE NEW BOOK OF KNOWLEDGE is a rich source of carefully selected photographs, drawings, art work, and diagrams—many in exciting, accurate full color.

As he picture-reads, your child handles books. He learns that we turn pages from right to left as we start to read from the front of a book. He learns to read from left to right and from the top of the page to the bottom.

Your Child's Knowledge Grows as You Read to Him

Man differs from all other living creatures in his ability to learn through indirect experiences. Through reading we conquer time and space, and we reach out beyond our physical limits. We help our youngsters understand this when we read aloud to them.

You can read aloud without being an actor. Fortunately, children make a warmly appreciative audience. A little practice and a few hints should make you a fine reader.

Read a selected story or poem to yourself first so you will understand it, feel its mood, and tailor your reading tone to the mood of the selection. Remember, too, that there is no one kind of story or poem or subject of an article that everyone must like. Tastes differ. A child's present interests determine the kind of story or poem he likes now. With time, growth, and guidance, his interests will widen, and so will his taste.

Children like to be read to for many reasons. They delight in your individual attention. They enjoy humor. They like to identify themselves with a brave hero or heroine. They want to extend their understandings of the world around them. They want to distinguish between fact and fancy. They are interested in hearing about the people who do the world's work and how we all help one another. They want to know about other ways of living in other places and other times. They particularly want to know how children live across the borders of space and time. They want to find out how to do things and why things are as they are.

Home Activities in Reading and Literature

Reading to your youngster is your early invitation to share the mysteries of the printed page with you. How proud he'll be when, after completing his first preprimer or primer, he brings it home to share with you. He both wants and needs your attentive audience. He may need some help with troublesome words. Encourage him by accepting his achievement, however simple it may seem to you. His teacher will correct his faults and encourage him to move along as fast as he can.

▶ HOW YOUR CHILD LEARNS TO READ

Teachers know that there are many ways to teach reading. No one way is best for all children or for any child at all times. That's why teachers use many methods and many materials.

Sight vocabulary. Most children begin to read by learning a sight vocabulary. These are simple words that your child learns to recognize on sight.

Phonics. Another method is the use of phonics. This is the association of speech sounds with a letter or a group of letters. Later, your child will learn to identify words by dividing them into their structural parts. This technique is useful in identifying longer and more difficult words.

Context. Your child will learn new words by their context in a sentence. The surrounding words and pictures tell your child the meaning of the new word.

Experience charts. Your child's teacher may ask children to dictate sentences describing an experience, an activity, or a story which she prints on the blackboard or on a chart. When children read these sentences they learn to recognize words common to their own experiences.

Basal readers. Most schools build the beginning reading program around a series of basal readers. These are graded books that have the special function of teaching reading.

Work books and programed materials. The basal readers are often supplemented by work books and programed materials. This type of material uses small sections or "frames" of reading content followed by a question, a direction, or a blank space to fill in. Thus, your child works at his own speed.

Individualized reading. A program of personal, or individualized, reading is also carried on by the school in connection with the how-to-read program. Your child selects books related to his own interests.

Initial Teaching Alphabet. Some schools teach reading by means of an experimental alphabet called the Initial Teaching Alphabet (i/t/a). This alphabet has 44 symbols, or characters. The 44 i/t/a symbols include the 26 letters of the English alphabet. Each symbol represents a sound that is always pronounced the same way. By the time your child reaches the third grade, he should be able to switch easily to the traditional alphabet.

Reading Problems

Your child's teacher will watch for signs of reading difficulty. She will take steps to help a child before the problem becomes a block to progress. She recognizes that some children have ear or eye defects that are not detected before they enter school. Sometimes reading instruction is begun before a child is "ready." Some young children cannot distinguish between sounds and words that are similar.

Many schools now provide special reading teachers trained to make diagnoses and provide corrective help for children who have reading problems. If you feel that your child requires special help, go to the teacher or principal who can advise appropriate action.

How You Can Help Your Preschool Child

When you read aloud to your preschool child you are providing the best preparation for learning to read in school.

Answer your child's questions and tell him what a word is if he is curious about it.

Recent research shows that young children who have been taught the letters of the alphabet at home may learn to read more quickly in school.

▶ **SPELLING**

Your child learns to spell after he knows how to read and write. The words he learns are those he needs to express his ideas in writing. Spelling learned for a real purpose is not easily forgotten.

The teacher knows that until your child can read a first reader easily and attack new words independently, it is not wise to emphasize spelling. However, readiness for spelling begins in the earliest grades. Your child examines alphabet books. He learns to identify letters. He learns alphabetical sequence by singing alphabet songs and playing alphabet games. Your child learns to make and use a picture dictionary. He learns to duplicate letters of the alphabet and to play spelling games like Word Lotto.

Systematic instruction in spelling is begun when your child has a large enough reading vocabulary, when he can write in manuscript, and when he can copy words correctly.

STORIES, FAIRY TALES, FABLES, MYTHS, AND LEGENDS

READING AND LITERATURE

POEMS, NURSERY RHYMES, AND SONGS

▶WRITING

As oral expression takes permanent form on paper and becomes writing, children learn to express their ideas and feelings in written language that others can read easily.

Teachers realize that children write best when they have something to say and a reason for saying it on paper. Your child's "Dear Santa" letter is readable because he has a reason for writing clearly. In school your child will write simple labels, signs, charts, and letters as he needs them in his school day. He'll probably use manuscript writing at first because it is easier to read and write, and resembles the printed words in his books. Toward the end of the second grade, or sometimes not until the third grade, your child will usually change over to the connected writing we call "cursive."

His teacher will encourage pride in legibility. As soon as he is ready, she will teach him proper page placement and letter formation. She will help him see that good writing requires proper physical balance. This means that his arm must rest comfortably on the desk and that his writing implements are comfortable to his little fingers and his limited physical ability. If your child is left-handed, his teacher will show him how to position his paper and use his left hand correctly.

Children develop clear, legible handwriting as they use it. Writing includes correct usage and spelling, and the ability to compose clear sentences and paragraphs. These skills take a long time to develop and require much practice. Writing is used in preparing a report, writing a letter of invitation or a story, in doing homework assignments, and in making a notebook. During the primary years your child will learn simple facts about these skills. Capitalization and punctuation will be taught as they are needed and used. Acceptable usage is taught as it is heard, for in these early grades "grammar" is taught largely by sound, rather than as a formal skill.

Creative Written Expression

Most children love to express their feelings, ideas, and experiences through talk. If properly encouraged they will enjoy expressing themselves in writing too. By creating a warm and friendly atmosphere, by encouraging youngsters who want to share creative poems, stories, and reports, teachers develop creative writing in school. They respect children's creative efforts and present them with dignity and respect.

The poems composed lovingly for Mother's or Father's Day or a birthday are also examples of creative writing. Encourage such efforts, and show your appreciation. Even though your child may never be a professional writer, creative writing, like music and art, offers him another path to self-expression and enjoyment.

WRITING

THE SOCIAL STUDIES, OR SOCIAL SCIENCES

The social studies (also called the social sciences) are the study of people and how they live. These studies include geography, history, government, economics, citizenship education, anthropology, and sociology. Naturally, in the earliest grades none of these individual disciplines will be identified by name. In fact, your child will seldom realize that he is learning any of the social sciences, while he is actually building the foundation for these studies in later grades.

Learning that he belongs to a family group was your child's first social studies lesson. Your youngster learns—after a time—that "belonging" also brings with it responsibility for others, and that it means people depending upon one another.

Gradually your youngster learns that his family is part of a larger family—the community. During his school years he will learn about his own community and about the larger communities—his state and region, the nation and the world. As he does this, he sees that just as membership in a family entails responsibility and caring for others, so does membership in the city, state, nation, or world.

Children have a deep sense of morality, nourished by their experiences with the adults around them. Although he may not always understand your words, your child does understand the feelings behind your interest in the daily news and in the problems of other people.

Children Learn Social Studies in Many Ways

As your youngster gathers information from many sources—people, projects, experiences, displays, pictures, and printed materials—he acquires understandings and facts that must be put together. In school, his teacher will present the larger meanings behind facts. She will help your child develop important concepts. She will teach him how and where to find the facts and how he can best use them.

His teacher will excite your child's imagination in many ways, using different materials and methods. She may bring an antique spinning wheel to school when the children are studying pioneer life. Letters from children in faraway lands add both fun and fact as they show similarities and differences of peoples around the world. A doll can tell much about how people dress or work. Stamp collections, photographs, slides, films, books, and realia supplement the information found in textbooks and reference books. Used wisely, both at home and in school, such resources extend a youngster's understanding of other people and other times.

Your child's teacher may take her class on educational trips—to the post office or a farm or the zoo. Through such actual contact, children learn how social institutions and organizations work—how people work together. A local policeman may come into the classroom to talk about traffic rules and the reasons for them. A postman may tell how letters are delivered, and a fireman may discuss fire prevention. The school bus driver may explain safety rules.

Films, filmstrips, opaque projectors, transparencies, pictures, and picture postcards all illuminate the study of times, places, and people. Perhaps the most important visual aids are the illustrations in children's books. The illustrations—photographs, art work, diagrams, and maps in THE NEW BOOK OF KNOWLEDGE have been selected carefully so that children will understand both the idea and the feeling behind them.

Often the right story or poem explains an idea in social studies with crystal clarity. THE NEW BOOK OF KNOWLEDGE has a rich supply of stories, legends, and poems for the kindergartener and primary grader.

SOCIAL STUDIES IN KINDERGARTEN AND THE PRIMARY GRADES

Social studies is the study of man and his relationship to his environment. Through social studies your child's teacher helps him prepare to live as a democratic citizen in an ever-changing world. She helps your child acquire basic knowledge and understanding of the world in which he lives. She guides him in the development of worthwhile attitudes toward other people. She helps him to attain skill in study and work habits, in social living, in problem solving, and in critical thinking. And she teaches your child to appreciate his American heritage, its values, and its ideals.

These are objectives of all education, not merely of the social studies. The teacher knows that school is only one avenue by which your child will attain these worthwhile attitudes, skills, and habits. She relies on the home to supplement the school.

In the earliest grades, teachers and parents working together can help young children achieve these objectives by:

Teaching children to live, work, and play together at home, in school, and in the community.

Teaching young children that people everywhere help one another, and that many people help us by supplying the services and goods that we need.

Teaching children that just as we have our ways of living, working, and playing, so people in other lands have theirs.

The following social studies topics are part of the kindergarten-to-third grade curriculum in most elementary schools. They lend themselves ideally to additional learning at home under guidance.

Homes and Families

"Home" is a special word that brings up an image of family living. Your child knows its meaning. As soon as he is able, he visits his neighbors' homes. It isn't long before he knows that people live in many different kinds of homes. With his father he may watch a house being built in the neighborhood. At home he may build a playhouse with blocks. Perhaps he helps his father repair a household appliance, or paint a room, or build bookshelves.

During his early school years he will learn about other people who live in quite different dwellings. He may learn how people live in hot desert regions, in the cold Arctic, or in a tropical rain forest. And he will learn about animal homes and families too, as he watches a mother cat care for her kittens, or a robin carrying worms to its young in a nearby nest.

Your child knows that home is a place of comfort and love. He knows, too, that families live and work together in their homes. He sees Mother create the feeling of a home. He shares the family work when he is able to help set the table or dry the dishes, when he tidies his room and puts his toys away, when he helps his father in the garden or takes care of his tools, and when he walks the dog or feeds the cat.

Families have fun together, and your child learns from these experiences too. Picnics, visits to the zoo, story reading time, ice-skating, swimming, listening to records, playing games together, sharing a hobby like stamp or coin collecting—all these are educational as well as recreational experiences.

HOME AND FAMILY LIFE

Animal homes	H273
Building materials	H171–75
Colonial home life	C385–99; H180–81
City housing	C309–10
Eskimo homes	F286–87
Family life	F37–43; A302–03
Family responsibility	F40–41
Farm life	F48–54
Grass houses	H172
Homes around the world	H168–84
Housing projects	R112; H182–83

Our School and Neighborhood

One of the most difficult tasks that the young school child faces is getting along with other children and adults. He soon learns that everyone must follow rules if people are to live and work together happily. The way he feels about himself and other people and the attitudes he has learned from you will shape his adjustment.

As he rides the school bus or walks to school or church or the neighborhood store, he learns where his friends live, what happens in different community buildings, what streets and roads are dangerous to cross and where the traffic lights and friendly policeman are. He carries a mental map of his home-school neighborhood.

During the primary years children gather in groups as they play in the school yard or playground. They sing songs and play games you knew when you were young. A bit later many join Cub Scouts, Brownies, Y's and Boys' and Girls' Clubs, as they seek well-rounded and guided group play.

THE COMMUNITY AND NEIGHBORHOOD

Days We Celebrate

Seasons and holidays are very important in a young child's life. By sharing in festivities with children at school, with others of his family, and with the community, your child links himself with his cultural and national heritage.

Birthdays, Mother's Day, Father's Day, Valentine's Day, Halloween, Thanksgiving, and Christmas are days for observance at home as well as in school. Celebrations are a time for sharing.

There is a tendency to decry the commercialism that characterizes holidays today. Parents should not allow this to interfere with their own family observance and celebration. Family holidays that commemorate happy events—even trivial events—are valuable learning experiences for children. Parents can help young children acquire a sense of obligation to remember others with thoughtfulness and kindness on birthdays, anniversaries, and holidays.

Patriotic holidays introduce children to our country's history and heritage. The American flag displayed at home as well as at school can mark an event or the birthday of a hero, and be the inspiration for family storytelling, reading, or singing.

Many articles in THE NEW BOOK OF KNOWLEDGE describe interesting activities that can help parents as well as teachers observe holidays. Some of the articles listed below provide background information. Others are "How to Make" and "How to Do" articles.

HOLIDAYS AND DAYS WE CELEBRATE

▶ INDIANS

Once upon a time other people lived in this part of the world, and they did not live as we do. Since your primary grader has little notion of past time, his interest in American history will be quite simple. But an introduction to the life of American Indians who once lived where he lives may start him on the path to better understanding of the people of the world, today and yesterday. The articles listed below suggest a wealth of pictures and text.

INDIANS

MATHEMATICS

By the time your child enters school he has had many experiences with numbers. He knows the number of his house. He knows that numbers are used for telephoning and for TV channels, and he knows how old he is. Your child recognizes the differences between coins even though he may not be sure of their actual value, and he has already learned something about fractions when he asks for half a cookie. Though his ideas of number may still be inaccurate, they furnish a starting point for your child's teacher.

Modern Mathematics

The modern mathematics program in elementary schools has undergone great changes in the past few years. In modern mathematics, the classroom is a laboratory containing materials that children can handle and use for experimentation. Modern mathematics emphasizes the development of concepts and logical thinking. Instead of relying on memorization of numbers, tables, and rules, modern mathematics teaches children to discover mathematical relationships. Basic facts and techniques of computation are mastered for the purpose of solving problems.

Your Child's Classroom

Walk into your child's classroom and look around. You'll probably see toy trucks, dolls, blocks, and an abacus. You may see dominoes and play money. These are called experience materials. You will also probably see place-value cards, disks, tens frames, and squared materials. These are called representative materials, because they are concrete representations of abstract numbers. Instruments of measure will include a real clock, a tape measure, a yardstick, a real thermometer, and transparent containers to measure pints and quarts.

Your Child's Teacher

Using many materials and many methods, your child's teacher introduces your youngster to mathematical concepts from the earliest grades. Experiences are an excellent means of developing mathematical concepts. A tape measure helps a child measure the cardboard "store" he builds. Play money is changed into smaller denominations. A clock with movable hands stands ready to teach time. Your child is taught to compute mentally, to find solutions by using a variety of methods, and to explain his reasoning to the class. He is encouraged to "estimate" the answer before solving a mathematical problem and then to compare the answer with his original estimate. He is introduced to the idea of "sets" and the "set theory."

How You Can Help Your Child with Mathematics

Even your first grader will occasionally bring home mathematics "homework." This is usually a page from his workbook. His teacher may ask him to complete an unfinished page at home. As he fills in, or colors, or marks the items on his work sheet, ask him to explain what he is doing and why.

Concepts, understandings, and skills in mathematics are cumulative. If your child does not understand one mathematical concept he may find difficulty in mastering a new one. Ask your child's teacher how you can help him at home.

Out of school experiences are an excellent means of developing mathematical understandings. Your child practices mathematics when he helps you plan a birthday party. How many children will he invite? How many invitations will he need, and what will the stamps cost? How many favors, cakes, cups, plates, and balloons shall he buy? How much change should he expect?

Help your child understand words like little and big, inch and foot, pint and quart, teaspoon and tablespoon. Provide him with a ruler to measure his growth against a mark on the wall. Help him to estimate the cost of single items when he goes to the supermarket with you.

The teacher uses similar experiences as the starting point for teaching mathematics. You can help your child in the same way. Learned this way, mathematics has more meaning for children and so is easier to understand and to learn.

SCIENCE

Although you may hold no teaching certificate, you've probably been teaching your youngster science since he first toddled after a butterfly or watched you bake a cake. When you showed him how to feed the goldfish, or pick up a kitten, or plant his own seeds in a windowbox, you were teaching him about the world of living things and about the rhythmic changes of life. As you shared your enthusiasm and encouraged his interest, you introduced him to scientific methods of learning and using knowledge.

There are many ways by which you teach your child science.

Observation. You teach your child to learn by observation when you stand at the window to see how the stars twinkle or watch the snow fall.

Doing. You teach him to learn by doing when you collect leaves and help him see the differences in size and shape, or when you let him hold a seashell to his ear so he can hear its curious sound.

Experimentation. You teach him to learn by experiment when you pop corn, or change a fuse, or use a lever to move a heavy object.

Scientific knowledge. You teach your child to use scientific knowledge when you read the thermometer to see whether he should wear a heavy sweater, or when you help him build a picnic fire and teach him the proper precautions.

Science in the Primary Grades

During his early school years your child will begin to understand about himself, about the world of living and nonliving things, and about the forces of nature surrounding him. His teacher will teach him to use simple scientific methods of thinking and acting. She will help him to recognize that science affects our ways of living, thinking, feeling, and doing; and that scientific knowledge carries with it certain responsibilities. She will help him to realize that all people depend on each other and upon plants and animals.

Your child will learn something about weather and how it affects our lives. He will begin to learn about the living things that move in the air. He will learn about sound and electricity and magnets; about the sun, the stars, and the moon; and about machines that help us travel and communicate with each other.

The following references in THE NEW BOOK OF KNOWLEDGE will help you meet or whet your child's science curiosity. They will help you answer the questions children often ask. The pictures will help your youngster understand many things even though he may not be ready to read the printed explanations. Because children usually learn best by doing, many activities are included—things for parent and child to do together for fun as well as for information.

You will know best how much information to share with your child, and the right time for sharing. The references in THE NEW BOOK OF KNOWLEDGE can help you help your child to discover the wonders and the joys of science.

SCIENCE

Articles in THE NEW BOOK OF KNOWLEDGE that describe specific animals and plants are too numerous to be listed here. Information can be found in the Index under the name of the particular animal or plant.

ART AND MUSIC

Your child began to enjoy art and music long before he reached school age. You introduced him to aesthetic experiences when you sang nursery songs and lullabies; when you played singing and dancing games. You stimulated him when you shared pictures with him and when you encouraged his early efforts by giving him the materials he needed and the appreciation he wanted.

Art

When your child starts school he already has a background of creative experiences. Your child's teacher encourages him so that he feels free to express his ideas through many art media. In school he will have access to a variety of materials. He will use bright-colored poster and finger paints, chalks, and crayons; and clay, paper, and fabrics of different textures. Because his teacher knows that large muscles must be developed during early school years, she encourages your child to work with large sheets of paper, large brushes, and thick crayons.

There are developmental stages in the use of art materials as in all learning. Your child needs time to explore and to manipulate art media before attempting representation. His teacher does not impose adult standards or techniques on him. She knows that young children get satisfaction from merely experimenting with materials and may not always make a finished product.

Your child's teacher will encourage him to experiment with a variety of brushstrokes. She knows that copying and filling in outlines are not creative art experiences. Dependence on prescribed outlines thwarts a child's creative instincts and prevents him from expressing himself with freedom and satisfaction.

You can help your child develop his creative ability at home. Help him to see that he has experiences and ideas worth expressing. Don't ridicule his efforts. Along with paper, blunt scissors, crayons, clay, chalk, pencils, and paint, give him scraps of colored cloth, string, yarn, bottle corks, empty spools, feathers, ribbons, beads, and paste. Provide a table to work on, a large square of plastic or oilcloth to catch the spills, one of Daddy's old shirts to use as a smock, and an easel or piece of wallboard to help him use new media and methods.

Display the results of his work but do not expect his art products to be easily recognizable, and do not ask him "What is it?" Instead, encourage him to talk about his art efforts when he wishes to. Don't set too high a standard of accomplishment or tell him how to express his ideas.

ARTS AND CRAFTS

Clay modeling	C336–37
Collage	C376–77
Finger painting	F126–28
Indian beadwork	I 157–59
Japanese flower arranging	J49–53
Making a color wheel	D139
Making a jewelry box	I 223
Making a place mat	I 224
Making greeting cards	G374
Making puppets and marionettes	P534–39
Making toys	T233–34
Making wrapping paper	I 224
Planning a party	P87–89
Origami	O222–26
Paper chromatography	E366
Papier-mâché	P58–59
Soap sculpture	S216–17; E366
Weaving	W97–98
Woodworking	W229–34

Music

Young children sing spontaneously. They imitate the sounds of cars, trains, boats, and planes. They may not be able to carry a tune but they enjoy singing nursery rhymes, nonsense songs, and songs about holidays, seasons, and home.

Your child's teacher uses music throughout the day. She will use phonograph records. She may play the piano and even a guitar, an accordion, or a recorder. Your child sings, listens to music, engages in rhythmic exercises and dramatic play, and even plays simple rhythm instruments.

You can encourage your child to love music. The phonograph records you buy and the radio and TV programs you select provide opportunities for the whole family to enjoy and appreciate music. Children's concerts and operettas are often featured in larger metropolitan areas. Family "sings" on holidays introduce children to traditional and seasonal music, and religious music in houses of worship provides an opportunity for children to sing with others.

MUSIC

Circle games	G13–17
Folk and square dances	F297–301
Folk music instruments	F329–30; G409–10
Folk songs	F318–28, 303–04
Hymns	H309–13
Lullabies	F303–04, 326
Musical instruments	M544–50; W182–83; S438–39; P151–53
Musical instruments for rhythmic experiences	
Bells	P153; B134–37
Castanets	P152
Cymbals	M550; P152
Drums	D333–36; M549–50; P151–52
Glockenspiel	P153; M550
Percussion instruments	P151–53; M544, 549–50
Tambourine	D335; P152
Triangles	M550; P152
Xylophone	M550; P153
National anthems and patriotic songs	N15–27
Nonsense and play party songs	F323–24
Seasonal songs	F324–26
Singing games	G11–13; F322
Spirituals	N105–07, 93; H313; F324

HEALTH AND SAFETY

School helps to keep your child safe and healthy. Each morning your child's teacher checks his appearance for signs of illness. Ears, eyes, teeth, height, and weight are checked at regular intervals.

Your child learns the importance of taking care of his own health and of being considerate of the health of others. School activities are planned so that physical activity is alternated with periods of relaxation.

Your child's safety is an important concern of the school. The safe way to use materials and equipment, to cross the street, to play after school, are constantly emphasized.

You can help your child by setting an example of good health and safety practices at home, and by explaining the reasons for these. Teach him to avoid accidents by obeying traffic, water safety, and fire prevention rules. Encourage him to practice good personal habits of nutrition and cleanliness.

HEALTH AND SAFETY

GAMES, TRICKS, AND PUZZLES

MEET THE OLDER ELEMENTARY SCHOOL CHILD

The older elementary school child can be wonderful to teach. This is an age of balance and calm compared to the earlier period of transition from home to school that marks the primary years; or compared to the later period of stress that marks the teens.

Your child in grades four, five, and six is interested in the world around him. The school not only tries to answer this interest, it also tries to broaden and deepen understandings sparked by your child's needs and enthusiasms.

Because of his interest in the adult world, the fourth-, fifth-, or sixth-grader fits in well with family schedules and plans. He cherishes his sense of growing independence, yet he wants and accepts limits. He hates to be bossed, but he responds to courteous treatment. He is eager to find his place in his own age group. He loves to conform, to belong to a team, a group, or a club. He may pursue such an interest for weeks or forget all about

it in a day. Each youngster works out his needs in his own way, if we allow him opportunity for choice and selection.

Your youngster loves to help plan family projects, trips, hobbies, and yes, even jobs that can be done together. He enjoys the wonderful feeling of companionship and the prestige his appreciated efforts bring.

Your older elementary school child is eager to know what things are, how they work, how they were discovered, and how they are used. He has great need to understand the meaning behind the facts and to see their connections. He collects things with enthusiasm. He may collect bottle tops, coins, stamps, marbles, minerals—or any of a hundred other things. Through these collections your youngster reaches out to learn about the world around him.

While many children pass from interest to interest as they go through the grades, any worthwhile enthusiasm can open new doors of understanding at different times. Butterflies are gay and pretty to watch when one is four or five; they may be fun for a second-grader to catch in a homemade net; but the fifth-grader may enjoy mounting and identifying them.

Essays or reports demanding the ability to generalize may pose problems, and your child may need your help. But if he is asked to write about the dog he trained or the tropical fish he raises, he'll surprise you with lively descriptions filled with carefully observed details. He may even wish to draw pictures to illustrate his report, for he is very anxious to share exact meanings.

You can use your youngster's interest in the specific as you help him develop reading skills and a respect for accuracy. You can help him use the tools and techniques of learning if you remember that children differ and therefore, that they learn differently. One youngster may require a great deal of help. Another may merely need a clue or suggested reference. A third may prefer to find his own way without your assistance. Censure or comparisons may foster feelings of inadequacy in your child, for confidence stems from gradual achievement. Being a fourth-,

fifth-, or sixth-grader isn't always easy. There are standards to be met at home, at school, in the neighborhood, and in the special world of one's own feelings. Confidence comes slowly, and children need help in developing it.

Older elementary school children may become lost in a maze of details. Help your child organize and review what he has learned. Teachers do this; they help select the important facts and ideas in any study. When called upon, you can help your child arrange and organize information, materials, and assignments. Of course, you won't always be successful. Some youngsters welcome an occasional suggestion. Some prefer to have their teachers, not their parents, suggest methods. And some youngsters just can't or won't organize the way parents wish they would. Gentle suggestions at the right time without "pushing" may in time bear satisfying fruit. There is always time.

There are many ways you can help your child indirectly, too. You can help him at home. A carefully planned party can be a lesson in learning to "follow through." Your youngster will let you know how much responsibility he can or will assume and what limits he needs.

LANGUAGE ARTS

Children read with many purposes. Some seek knowledge of people, places, and things. Some find comfort as they read about children like themselves. Sometimes children read for fun and pleasure, or just to while away the time.

No one type of reading matter or story appeals to all youngsters. There are stories that strike the spark of enthusiasm in a child and start him on his reading way. Some youngsters prefer fairy tales; others like science fiction, adventure stories, or animal stories. Whatever kind of story your child reads, he is living vicariously—traveling in a time machine to other places and times, and into the minds and hearts of other people.

Librarians and Teachers Encourage Reading

Both librarians and teachers are dedicated to the task of helping children find the right reading material at the right time. Your child's teacher may try to capture his interests:

By having library times when children may read for fun.

By displaying books attractively, making them hard to resist.

By encouraging book reviews and reports, not just to see if the child has read the story, but rather to share reactions to good stories.

By appointing a library committee so children can check their own books in and out as they use the class card catalog.

By allowing time for "book talk." Shared enthusiasm sparks reading faster than anything else.

By taking the class to the school library or the public library regularly.

By finding a special story for a certain child.

Most of all, by sharing her own delight in reading.

While both librarians and teachers try to capture your child's enthusiasm for reading, encouraging lifetime reading habits is largely the business of the home. Here is where parents can really help their children.

Parents Encourage Reading at Home

Parents who enjoy reading can share their pleasure by reading to very young children. But the older elementary school child also needs to hear stories read to him. Perhaps he needs this experience in the fourth through sixth grades more than he did before, for Scouts, sports, clubs, hobbies, music lessons, and myriad other activities take up his time and energy.

Help your child find the kind of story that interests him. His interests will expand and change from time to time. Explore the lists of stories in THE NEW BOOK OF KNOWLEDGE, found at the end of this Guide. The HOME AND SCHOOL READING GUIDE that accompanies your set of THE NEW BOOK OF KNOWLEDGE lists recommended books according to subjects in the encyclopedia. Your school or community library will suggest books and book lists to meet your child's interests. Encourage the habit of reading aloud to other members of the family.

▶THE NEW BOOK OF KNOWLEDGE—A BRIDGE TO WIDER READING

Not all youngsters read equally well, nor do they all read the same kind of story. One outstanding value of THE NEW BOOK OF KNOWLEDGE is the inclusion of excellent stories for different reading levels and tastes.

Teachers know that the more a youngster reads and enjoys, the more he will want to read. Getting started is sometimes difficult for the older elementary-grader who has not read very much before. Some reading authorities suggest that such children be encouraged to read simple stories that interest them, until they gain the confidence they need. With each successful reading experience, your child becomes a more competent as well as a more confident reader. If he reads a story and enjoys it, it has meaning for him.

THE NEW BOOK OF KNOWLEDGE can help parents provide a bridge to wider reading. Often children just don't know what they want to read. Browsing through THE NEW BOOK OF KNOWLEDGE will help them discover many possibilities. As a child handles the volumes, spotting stories that he likes, you can help him expand his reading by finding other stories in THE NEW BOOK OF KNOWLEDGE and in other books at home.

Help him become acquainted with the inexhaustible storehouse of good reading in the local public library. And finally, help him to build up his personal library by gifts of books from time to time.

Reading is Thinking

During grades four, five, and six, your child will be taught to think as he reads. Training in thoughtful reading does begin in the primary grades. But during the older elementary school grades, both general reading skills and special reading skills are emphasized.

Your child will learn to find information in libraries, in books, in chapters, on pages, and in paragraphs. And he'll learn how to use the appropriate sources of information.

Reading growth is a complex process. Teachers remember that each child is an individual with differences that affect his reading. Therefore, they tailor reading instruction to the child's needs and purposes. Strong supplementary support at home can be most effective when parents and teachers work together.

How You Can Help Your Child Improve His Reading

Understand that reading skills improve slowly but surely as they are used and as children grow and develop. Encourage your child by providing opportunities to use his reading skills. Help him develop the habit of seeking information in reference books. Encourage his enthusiasm and interests.

See that your child wears glasses if he needs them. Provide him with a quiet place where he can work, read, and do his home assignments. See that he has a good reading light and a comfortable chair and desk.

Encourage and appreciate his efforts and accomplishments. Share his interests and enthusiasms in what he has read or is working on.

Provide him with a basic collection of suitable reference books so that his needs for information can be satisfied as they arise. THE NEW BOOK OF KNOWLEDGE can be the foundation of such collection. A suitable dictionary, an annual almanac, an atlas, a yearbook, and a globe are a few of the useful reference tools that can help your child improve his reading skills and develop the habit of reading for information.

▶ READING SKILLS

In grades four, five, and six your child will learn and improve many reading skills. He will learn:

To use the dictionary for word meaning and to expand his vocabulary.

To recognize word structure.

To tackle new words by breaking them into syllables and by guessing the meaning of the word through its familiar parts.

To think critically as he reads.

To distinguish between fact and opinion.

To use different speeds for different reading purposes.

To outline and take notes as he reads.

To use the parts of a book—table of contents, index, glossary, footnotes, chapter and paragraph headings, guide words.

To select the right book for a particular purpose.

Your child's teacher will help him with the particular reading skills he needs to improve. Ask her how you can help at home. The foundations of reading were laid in earlier grades. But reading skills must be used and expanded as children grow in their ability to use them.

Reading is a vital part of the entire school program. It is taught all day long, as children use different kinds of printed materials.

LITERATURE

READING

REFERENCE AND RESEARCH

▶ **WRITTEN EXPRESSION**

Writing means handwriting, correct usage, spelling, and composing clear sentences and paragraphs. Children must express themselves in writing when they make a report, write a letter or invitation, do homework, take notes, create stories, or review books. Parents and teachers can encourage children by creating an atmosphere conducive to good writing.

Formal Writing

In writing invitations, thank-you notes, homework assignments, reports, minutes, and letters asking for information, children learn that there are certain acceptable forms and usages for each type of written expression.

Formal grammar is generally not taught directly in elementary grades, but correct usage is taught as part of the planned program and informally throughout the school day when the need arises.

Parents can help children use acceptable language by using correct forms themselves. When you write a letter, a list, or a note to the teacher you can observe the correct and acceptable form and usage that youngsters are urged to adopt. Provide children with opportunities for using correct written forms at home. Help your youngster write the invitations to a party, a thank-you note for a gift, or a letter to a friend or relative. There are many opportunities for intelligent practice at home.

But your child must know that there is a reason for writing.

Creative Writing

Just as children learn at school to express themselves in acceptable formal written language, so they learn to write creatively. Creative writing (stories, poems, plays, and reports of experiences, feelings, and observations) gives children a channel of expression and a chance to sharpen and share their perceptions. Many children love to write creatively if they receive encouragement.

Perhaps you have never encouraged creative writing knowingly at home. But you can. The important ingredient is your response. When your youngster describes an experience with excitement, you might say, "That would make an exciting story. I'd love to see you write it."

Provide your youngster with the encouragement of a truly accepting audience. And share your own creative efforts, too. Some families play storytelling games. Others collect special stories, riddles, and jokes to tell at dinner. There are many ways. But an attentive audience and an accepting atmosphere are two important elements needed if children are to write creatively.

▶ **SPELLING**

By the end of grade six, your child will probably have a writing vocabulary of about 3,000 words. These words have been learned functionally, as well as from graded spelling lists that are based on national research.

In grades four, five, and six, your child will learn to use a dictionary for word definitions, pronunciation, and syllabication as well as for spelling. He will be taught to proofread his own writing for errors, and to keep his own list of the words he frequently misspells.

You can help your child by providing him with a suitable dictionary. Encourage him to use the dictionary, and to proofread his writing at home for spelling errors. Many educators believe there is a close correlation between legible handwriting and the ability to spell. Learning to type is also considered a good way to improve a child's spelling ability.

WRITING

The first article in each volume of THE NEW BOOK OF KNOWLEDGE describes a letter of the alphabet. Illustrating each of these letter articles is a model of the accepted form of that letter in both manuscript and cursive writing.

▶ORAL EXPRESSION

Children acquire their basic speech patterns, accents, and habits of enunciation from their parents and families, from their neighborhood friends, and from the speech of the region in which they live. Your child's speech pattern is largely formed by the time he starts school.

The school can do much, however, to improve speech habits by providing instruction in oral expression. Teachers and parents recognize that children speak and listen more frequently than they read and write. The teacher provides many opportunities for your child to practice oral expression. These range from making simple announcements to taking part in group discussions. In grades four through six children report on individual and group projects, tell about personal experiences, impart and explain information, give directions, answer questions, tell stories, recite poetry, engage in conversation, take part in dramatics and choral speaking, make introductions, conduct interviews, read aloud to the class, and dramatize telephone conversations.

How Parents Can Help

If your child needs remedial speech help, the school may either provide such trained attention or refer you to someone who is qualified to give it. If your child does not need special speech therapy, his oral expression can be encouraged and guided if you provide the opportunities.

Answering the telephone, ordering food, family conversation, and informal conversation with neighbors are all different kinds of talk. Your child should learn that we often talk differently for different occasions. Certain kinds of talk are appropriate in one situation and not in others. Children want to talk. Parents, by creating acceptance at home, can encourage good speech. There are many ways, but they all center around the habit of listening to what your child says, and accepting his verbal offerings with enthusiasm. At home, parents can encourage good speech by speaking well themselves; by avoiding interrupting the child to correct his speech, but by using the correct form soon after; and by respecting the child's right to an attentive audience.

▶ LISTENING

There is a direct relationship between the kind of speaking and reading that children do and the way in which they listen. Encouraging them to speak so that others can understand them will improve children's listening habits. Whatever teachers and parents can do to improve children's ability to listen with understanding also contributes to their ability to understand reading materials.

One of the best ways in which parents can encourage good listening is to listen courteously and attentively when children speak. Reading aloud to children encourages good listening habits. Listening to recordings, radio, television, and motion pictures offers wonderful opportunities to improve listening skills. Discussing what one has heard is an excellent way to make listening more purposeful.

If you want your child to learn to listen well, you might ask yourself the following questions: Do I talk in a way I'd like to hear if I were my child? Do I speak simply and to the point, or do I confuse my child with words and ideas he can't understand? Do I repeat the same message over and over so my child no longer wants to hear it? Do I address my child mostly when I want to scold, advise, or order? Do I address my child as courteously as I do my guests, or do I reserve polite language for strangers? The simple, natural courtesy you show your child and other members of the family is the most important factor in encouraging good listening habits.

SPEAKING AND LISTENING

SOCIAL STUDIES

Social studies in the upper elementary grades broadens your child's understanding of the world around him and strengthens his appreciation of his American heritage. The social studies curriculum in grades four through six varies from school to school. In general, however, your child will learn about his city and state; about the history and geography of the United States and other nations in the Western Hemisphere; about climatic regions, continents, and typical nations of the world; about America's historical and cultural roots in the Old World; and about the role of the United States in world affairs. He will learn about these broad topics through the study of history, biography, current affairs, political science, economics, and even anthropology.

Methods of teaching social studies vary from school to school. Your child may study the social studies disciplines as separate subjects—chiefly history and geography. In general, social studies will be taught through the study of major topics or units with such titles as Transportation, Life in the Polar Regions, How the United States Became an Industrial Nation, and so forth. Units based on topics of this kind may involve many subjects in the curriculum—science, language arts, mathematics, and music, for example, as well as all the aspects of the social studies. A unit may touch on many parts of the world and on many periods of history. Biography and literature, group projects and activities, trips and discussions, will all be used by your child's teacher to develop social studies concepts and to impart factual information.

Teachers Develop Children's Understandings, Concepts, and Skills

Whatever organization or method your child's teacher uses, she tries to help your child develop certain understandings, concepts, and skills. These include understanding our country's way of life; appreciating the events and people that influenced the history of our country; understanding the geographic influences that affect the ways people live; and understanding the techniques of research and problem-solving in the pursuit of information.

Social Studies Skills Begin in the Elementary Grades

Children cannot understand the past or the present without certain important study skills. We know that skills develop slowly as the child matures and becomes physically, emotionally, and mentally ready to use them. We know, too, that skills are developed gradually as they are needed and used.

In the upper elementary grades your child perfects his reading skills because reading is the basic skill on which much of his learning will depend.

He'll learn how to use maps, globes, and atlases. He'll interpret map symbols, the map index, and the legend. He'll construct maps, locate places, estimate distances, understand the relationship of places through direction, and interpret information on maps. He'll learn that there are many kinds of maps, and that maps can be used for special purposes.

Study skills are not limited to the social studies; they extend into other curriculum areas. Your child will learn to use the encyclopedia. This means learning to locate information by using the index and guide words. He'll learn to locate references to a topic by using bibliographies and the library card catalog. He will use the dictionary to find the meaning of a word, and so come to understand the special vocabulary of the social studies. He will learn to read graphs, charts, and diagrams. When he needs special information, he will learn how to write letters and to interview people. He will work on committees; use parliamentary procedure; participate in discussions; organize, prepare, and deliver oral and written reports; and write for his class or school newspaper.

Because the future of our nation and of the world depends upon intelligent and informed citizens, your child will study current affairs. Some classes subscribe to professionally prepared school newspapers designed for a particular grade level. Such newspapers present the news simply and graphically. Many schools use educational television and radio programs to stimulate current-affairs discussion. In many schools, people with special qualifications are invited to address children.

How Parents Can Help

You can help your child in social studies by understanding that not all children develop all skills at the same time, at the same rate, or with equal facility. Help your child find the information he needs, if he wants help. Help him find the special maps he needs. You use road maps and depend on them. Show your child how the scale and the legends on an automobile map help you determine your route. Let him take charge of the road map and direct the driver of the car on your next automobile trip.

Show him how to use reference books. Provide him with a good dictionary, an up-to-date atlas, and a globe; and help him to use these valuable tools. Teach him to use the daily newspaper and the weekly news magazine. Discuss important news events at the family table. Help your child distinguish between sensational gossip, unfounded rumor, and important current events. Personalize social studies. Try to tie in current events and ideas with his life by asking such questions as "Why is the United States interested in this question?" Show him that you care about your local and national government. Explore ways of extending your child's interest in history, government, social processes, and geography. Plan family trips to museums and historic places that illuminate his study. Make birthdays and holidays a time for giving books that will build up your child's personal library of informational resources.

There are many more ways of helping your child understand and enjoy social studies. Your sensitivity to your child's needs and interests will be the decisive factor.

PREHISTORIC TIMES

Ancient man	A306
Anthropology	A300–09
Archeology	A343–65
Art	P439–41; I 152–57
Cave drawings	P439–41, 14–15; C157–58, 430–31
Cave dwellers	P443; C157–58
Clothing, primitive	I 347; C348; F511
Communication	C430
Dinosaurs	D172–81; A263; F379; G200, 202, 204; L224
Earth's history	E18–21
Fire and early man	F138–45; P444
Food	F331; P442–43
Hunters and gatherers	P442; F141, 138–45; I 162–63
Ice ages	I 9, 13–24; L225, 237
Java man	S334; I 222; P442
Mammoths and mastodons	E338–40, 170; L337; M63, 578; P443
Neanderthal man	P443; E347
Old basketmakers	I 164
Old Bering Sea people	E284
Old bison hunters	I 163
Old millers	I 164
Peking man	P442; A3–8; F139
Prehistoric man	P442–46; I 163–64; A306
Speech, development of	C430
Stone ages	P442–46
Tools	T210; P443–44
Transportation	T257

MIDDLE AGES

Agriculture	F99–103; A96
Armor and coats of arms	A433–35; H115–18; K272
Art and architecture	A377; B435, 483–90; C131; D70–75; E191; G165–66; H178; I 458; M296–97; P17–18; S393–94; U45

AGE OF EXPLORATION AND DISCOVERY

FAMOUS SAYINGS

FAMOUS PEOPLE IN THE AMERICAN REVOLUTION

PIONEER LIFE AND WESTWARD EXPANSION

FAMOUS PIONEERS

UNITED STATES

THE FIFTY STATES OF THE UNITED STATES

THE NEW BOOK OF KNOWLEDGE describes the fifty states in a series of comprehensive articles prepared by experts in the states. Some schools study their state in the middle grades; some in the upper grades. The state articles in THE NEW BOOK OF KNOWLEDGE are written and organized so that your child can locate and select the exact information he needs for his particular grade.

Each state article is introduced with an exciting anecdote about the state. Each article is handsomely illustrated with many full color photographs. These include the state flag, tree, seal, bird, and flower as well as photographs of important aspects of the state's geography, economy, and places of interest. Fact boxes help your child find the exact information he needs. The many and varied maps that accompany each state article appear adjacent to the text information that relates to each map. Each state article is organized according to the following outline:

The land—landforms; rivers and lakes; climate; natural resources.

The people and their work—where they live; industries and products; transportation and communication.

Education—schools and colleges; libraries and museums.

Places of interest—parks, memorials, and other places of interest; annual events.

Cities—the capital city and other important cities.

Government.

Famous people: biographies of people associated with the state.

History.

The state's future.

STORIES ABOUT THE STATES

Each of the 50 state articles in THE NEW BOOK OF KNOWLEDGE is introduced by a story. The subjects are listed below.

CANADA

FAMOUS FIGURES IN CANADIAN HISTORY

NORTH AMERICA

COUNTRIES OF NORTH AMERICA

SOUTH AMERICA

Greece	G331–66, 95, 98, 123; A153, 171–73, 228–30, 246–47, 360, 374; B19, 153, 394, 435; C206–07, 285, 311, 431, 556–58; D23, 29, 35, 69–70, 293–94; E62–63; F2, 4–5, 239, 297, 340, 492; H104, 167, 178; I 169, 429, 430, 434, 435, 436; J93, 96; L76, 194; M203–04, 320; N7–8, 378–83; O53–54, 103–04, 165, 180; P16–17, 156, 191–92, 224, 332, 378, 414; R306–07; S61, 94, 195–96, 228; T293–94; W238, 275, 290
Hungary	H283–88; A525; C49, 444; D30; E325; F239, 340; L26
Iceland	I 41–45; E15, 274–75; F239; G192; N277; P436; S50–51; V339
Ireland	I 384–95; A97; C283, 284; D298–99; E222, 228, 232; F239, 266; G225; H43; L31–32; O51; P98, 411; R290; T161; U68, 69, 73, 78; V338; Y345
Italy	I 446–86, 428, 429, 437; A380–84, 387; B55–59, 134, 148, 341–42; D38, 352; E300; F63, 64, 239, 336, 341; G57, 229; L27, 28; M186, 391, 552; N20, 347; O130; P18, 20–21, 23, 378; R157–70, 312–17; S35–36, 98–99; T160, 196; U2–3; V280–82; W271–81, 284, 286, 297
Liechtenstein	L206–07; F239
Luxembourg	L379–80; F239; W288
Monaco	M406–07; F240
Netherlands	N115–21, 18–19, 225; B59–61; C292, 293, 349; D7, 12, 308, 363–65; E240, 244, 337, 341, 444, 505–06; G396–97; H18, 272–73; L31; M408; P23, 24, 512; R155–56, 172–73; V305; W88
Norway	N339–44, 277–81; A97; C349; E274–75, 306, 325; F22, 228, 240, 297, 341; G370–71, 376; I 2, 41, 44–45, 434, 437; L44–45; S49, 50–53, 152–54; V337–40
Poland	P358–62; B139; C444–45; D29; F240, 341; J109; W286
Portugal	P399–404; A67, 260–61; B383–84, 450; E374; F240; G7, 101; I 427, 428, 434; L49; M17, 500; R237; S197
Rumania	R355–60; B19; F240; W275
San Marino	S35–36; F240, 375
Spain	S350–76, 294–95; A254–55, 524–25; B59, 306, 499–51; C350, 550; D30, 77, 296; E57, 66, 178–79, 221–22; F64, 87, 227, 240, 343, 450; G279, 330; H101–03; I 257, 417–22, 427–28; J107; L49; M11–13, 17; N347; O101, 137; P23–24, 27, 406; U10; V294; W285–86
Sweden	S482–87; F240, 341; L44–45; M513; O98; P407; S50–53
Switzerland	S495–502; A174–75, 309; C97, 286, 350; E305, 327; F240; G102, 103, 178, 179, 224; H177; L28; M499; W50, 171
Turkey	T323, 324–25, 326, 327–29; B491–92 See also Turkey in Asia.
United Kingdom	U65–79; C428; E179, 212, 271; F339; G205, 277; H109, 148–49, 150, 152, 199–200, 203–05; I 390, 427, 428, 430, 435, 436, 437; J112–13; L32, 333–40; M301, 508; O98, 99; P81–82, 372–73, 378–79, 456, 483–84; R135, 248; S86–89; T159; W3–4
U.S.S.R.	U27–57; B25–26, I38–39; C442–45; E82; F341; H119–20; I 434, 436; K240–41; L26, 27, 32, 33, 138, 139–40; M464–67; N61; O98; P168, 477; R243, 244, 248; S173, 395; T408; U8–9
Vatican City	V280–82; F240; I 469; L197; R296, 298–99
Yugoslavia	V354–59; B19; C444, 445; F240, 299; T199

▶ MATHEMATICS

Modern mathematics in the upper elementary grades contains new subject matter, new ideas, and new ways of looking at old subject matter. Your child will continue to perfect his skills in the basic computational operations of mathematics—addition, subtraction, multiplication, and division of numbers. But he will be taught to apply new ideas and methods. These new ideas and methods run throughout all mathematics from kindergarten to college. Thus, in grades four, five, and six your child will continue to apply the set theory. He will learn about the associative and distributive properties of numbers. He will work with experience materials and representative materials as he did in earlier grades. And he will be taught to reason, to recognize mathematical relationships, and to solve problems.

THE NEW BOOK OF KNOWLEDGE articles listed below describe the most modern practices in mathematics. As a parent, you will find them invaluable in understanding your child's new mathematics program, and in helping him with his homework.

During the primary grades your child learned to see, to do, to try, to wonder, to question, to experiment, and to judge science phenomena. His enthusiasm helped to shape the science program. The teacher guided your child's efforts and encouraged him to use scientific methods of thinking.

During grades four, five, and six, teachers continue to encourage scientific curiosity and attitudes, while leading children to a systematic understanding of the importance of science information.

Science All Day

Science plays an important part in your child's school day. In school he learns that civilization continues to unfold as people progress in understanding their physical environment. He learns the importance of body health and muscular development. He learns that the sounds of music are composed of loudness, pitch, and quality. If he plants a school garden, he learns that plants need sun and water. He learns about volcanoes, earthquakes, glaciers, rivers, seas, the wind, man, and the other forces that continually change the surface of the earth.

Science will help your child understand the importance of community health and safety. He will learn about the relationship of the earth to the other heavenly bodies. He will discover that man adjusts to the changing climate and surface of the earth. He will learn that man depends on plants and animals and that he is responsible for their wise use and conservation. He will appreciate the many forms of energy that are used to improve man's way of living. And he will learn about some of the great men and women of science.

Science learning would be of little value to children if they did not apply it to daily living. That is why your child's teacher helps him to develop the following attitudes:

"I don't know, but let's find out." By using scientific methods of observation, research, and investigation, and by weighing evidence and forming judgments, your child sees that educated people want to learn. This attitude lies behind all scientific progress. An open mind is imperative in scientific thinking.

"Let's get the facts and use them." This attitude has saved and lengthened lives and eliminated disease. Basic facts about health and safety, cleanliness and diet, rest and proper clothing, and man's needs and obligations for the well-being of others are stressed in grades four, five, and six.

"What does this really mean?" Critical thinking helps youngsters weigh evidence, judge pertinent data, and determine the truth. What is fact? What is opinion? During grades four, five, and six, science can teach your child to recognize faulty thinking. Critical thinking can help your child see cause-and-effect relationships. Through science education, your child will learn to question, to think critically, to apply scientific methods, and to use science knowledge as he learns to adjust to his environment.

"How does science help us?" Your child will be taught to judge scientific discoveries in terms of their contributions to mankind. He'll learn that science helps us to live more comfortably, makes us healthier, and teaches us to think more clearly. It also helps us extend our ability to enjoy, to sympathize, and to feel secure. Learning about the unknown may help your child conquer his fear of it. When he learns to understand, protect, and love living things, he'll find increased comfort in the order of the universe.

"There's much to enjoy in life." One of the finest contributions that science can make to your youngster's life is that of increasing his pleasure in the living world around him. As enthusiasms expand, they bring your child greater pleasure in living and learning.

How Parents Can Help

You can help your older elementary school child develop the scientific attitudes, the open-mindedness, and the purposes his teacher is encouraging.

Stimulate his interests. Help him get the supplies and tools he needs.

Share your enthusiasms with him, for they are contagious. And share his enthusiasms, too.

Help him find and use appropriate sources of information (museums, government agencies, reference books, local nature experts).

Understand the important concepts, facts, and ideas your child's teacher is stressing. Find examples and experiments that illustrate these concepts.

Show him the science all around us—in the refrigerator, the TV, the air conditioner, the daily newspaper, the backyard.

Use scientific thinking yourself.

SCIENCE

HEALTH AND SAFETY

Your child's health and safety continue to be important concerns of his teacher in grades four, five, and six. Your child's cumulative health record follows him from grade to grade, and helps his teacher adjust her instruction to your child's individual needs.

Though health education is taught in connection with science, social studies, and language arts, planned units in health, safety, and physical education are also part of the program for upper elementary grades.

Your child continues to practice health and safety rules. He learns about first aid; good food and eating practices; body structure; care of teeth, eyes, and ears; the importance of sleep and rest; and the dangers of stimulants, narcotics, and tobacco.

In physical education your child will learn group games, folk dancing, and rhythmic activities. He will be taught to derive satisfaction from self-achievement rather than from competition.

How You Can Help

All parents want their children to be healthy. But good health is more than not being sick.

Food, exercise, and rest are only part of the health story. Teach your child the importance of safety rules, of hand-washing, of caring for his teeth, of sleep, and of exercise. Planning exercise for the fourth-, fifth-, or sixth-grader may seem foolish. To many parents, the problem appears to be the opposite. Yet it is sometimes necessary to see that your child exercises actively. He is more apt to like this if it comes under the heading of sports and play rather than exercise. Your child will benefit from physical activities if he is not pressured to engage in a particular sport or to become a star performer.

Physical activities which your child can use all his life are preferable. Swimming, ice-skating, dancing, tennis, skiing, and golf are all skills he can learn now and enjoy as an adult.

HEALTH AND SAFETY

▶ MUSIC

In grades four, five, and six, children begin to learn two-part songs, and even how to read simple music. As they listen to live or recorded musical performances, upper elementary graders learn to recognize and appreciate the various forms that music takes. Many children of this age experiment with musical instruments at home and also at school, where they often have an opportunity to play in a band or orchestra.

►ART

Art is an important school experience for your fourth-, fifth-, or sixth-grader, just as it was in earlier grades. In the upper elementary grades your child will paint, draw, model in clay, design posters, construct with wood, make puppets, and work with paper, cloth, and yarn. Much of his creative art work will be related to his personal experiences in and out of school and to other subjects in the curriculum.

You can add to your child's art experiences by referring to the beautiful color reproductions that illustrate the history of art articles listed below. In addition, THE NEW BOOK OF KNOWLEDGE contains many "How To" articles that will help to develop your child's artistic abilities and supplement his school craft work.

ART AROUND THE WORLD

African art	A70–76
Art in the United States	U115–27
Dutch and Flemish art	D349–62
Egyptian art and architecture	E92–103
English art and architecture	E233–43
French art and architecture	F421–32
German art and architecture	G165–71
Indian art of North and South America	I 152–57
Islamic art and architecture	I 417–22
Italian art and architecture	I 458–73
Latin-American art and architecture	L62–67
Oriental art and architecture	O212–19
Spanish art and architecture	S360–65
Russian art and architecture	U45–51

ARTS AND CRAFTS

Clay modeling	C336–37
Collage	C376–77
Finger painting	F126–28
Indian beadwork	I 157–59
Japanese flower arranging	J49–53
Leaf prints	L118
Making a color wheel	D139
Making a jewelry box	I 223
Making a loom	I 158–59
Making a place mat	I 224
Making greeting cards	G374
Making puppets and marionettes	P534–39
Making toys	T233–34
Making wrapping paper	I 224
Origami	O222–26
Papier-mâché	P58–59
Photography	P201–13
Planning a party	P87–89
Soap sculpture	S216–17
Weaving	W97–98
Woodworking	W229–34
Wrapping gifts	G206–09

RELATED ART ARTICLES

Animated cartoons	A297–99
Architecture	A370–87
Art	A437
Cartoons	C125–28
Design and color	D132–43
Drawing	D301–05
Graphic arts	G302–08
Mosaic	M463
Museums	M509–20
Hermitage Museum	H119–20
Louvre	L366–68
Metropolitan Museum of Art	M236–37
National Gallery (London)	N38–39
National Gallery of Art (Washington, D.C.)	N40–41
Prado	P428–29
Uffizi	U2–3
Obelisks	O5–6
Painting	P14–31
Perspective	P158–59
Posters	P404
Pottery	P413–19
Sculpture	S90–105

GRADES 7, 8, AND 9

There are moments when the parents of a teen-ager say, or at least think, "Why don't you act your age?" But what age is the young adolescent to act? One minute he is twelve years old; the very next he seems sixteen; and a moment later he reverts to childish behavior. The betwixt-and-between junior high school pupil offers his parents and teachers an exciting challenge, for adults cannot guide seventh-, eighth-, and ninth-graders without growing themselves.

These are years of rapid change. Your teen-ager's perplexities start with bodily changes. Almost as soon as the young teen-ager begins to understand and accept these physical changes, he has a different body to accept. His legs and arms seem to grow like weeds. Girls often become heavier and taller than boys of the same age, though this difference seems to level out at the end of the junior high school period. Along with rapid growth comes an increased appetite, or else finickiness about foods. The young teen-ager's skin may pose new problems, for his glands are working in new ways.

Most junior high school pupils have reached the age of puberty. Many accept these startling changes gracefully. Others worry excessively about their health and their bodies. They may translate their worries into aggressive or withdrawn behavior. Some youngsters may seem sluggish; others may exude energy. New croaking voices may seem unpredictable and shocking, and the adolescent boy may find it hard to believe that *this* voice came from his mouth. Girls may find their newly obvious breasts a source of embarrassment, and make ineffectual efforts to hide them. Others are quite proud of these signs of maturity. Adults can help young adolescents accept their new growth by helping them understand that what is happening to them is a perfectly natural part of growing up.

► REACHING FOR INDEPENDENCE

Physical changes color your young adolescent's emotions. He has been striving for independence since his childhood. This effort gains greater force during grades seven, eight, and nine. Strong, surging needs dominate his entire personality. These needs are:

The need to establish independence from adult authority.

The need to conform to the code of his peers, for his friends and their values are all-important to him.

The need to adjust to friends of his own sex, and to know how to behave with members of the opposite sex.

The need to accept himself as worthwhile.

Home, school, and community can help youngsters temper these urges and route them into healthy, acceptable channels.

Your young adolescent's need for independence shows itself in many ways. Some youngsters want part-time jobs. As he earns spending money or lives within his allowance, your growing child develops healthy attitudes toward work and money-management, especially if he is wisely guided by adults who have come to terms with similar problems. If he is occasionally allowed to make mistakes, he will learn from his own mismanagement. Through his need for independence and his interest in working, he begins to wonder "What shall I do when I grow up?"

► WHY YOUNG ADOLESCENTS ACT AS THEY DO

Just as his new physical growth affects the way your youngster feels, so it affects the way he acts. The boy wonders "What kind of man will I be?" The girl wonders "What's ahead for me?" They look to parents and teachers for guidance and for acceptance in the strange world of grownups. Your fourteen-year-old boy challenges his father to a swimming race or a game of tennis. Father, understanding his son's need to measure his maleness, hides his fatigue and resolves not to be beaten.

Your teen-age daughter, hitherto tractable and helpful, becomes suddenly rebellious. She may flatly refuse to tidy her room. She may ask "Why don't you act like other mothers do?" Or she may withdraw into her own world and become almost a stranger.

While imitating adult behavior at one moment, your young adolescent may at the next feel compelled to devise his own codes of behavior—codes that may be in direct conflict with adult standards. Your teen-ager experiments with many roles before he finds the personality that is his own. Because he feels a strong need to conform to his friends' standards, your son may say "Tom is allowed to go hunting; why can't I?" Mothers of adolescent girls are familiar with the refrain "Peggy is allowed to go to the movies during the week; why can't I?"

This is the golden age for organized clubs and groups. At the same time your young adolescent is principally concerned with himself. Wrapped up in his own hobbies, he often finds it difficult to appreciate his friends' different interests. He is intensely afraid of ridicule, though he has a splendid sense of humor. He is oversensitive and highly self-critical. Of course, children differ. But studies indicate that an overwhelming number of seventh-, eighth-, and ninth-graders show these characteristics.

► THINKING AND LEARNING

Along with his changing body, feelings, and actions, the young adolescent has new abilities and new ways of learning. His ability to think abstractly and to express his ideas has increased. He is fascinated by large concepts like justice, democracy, friendship, citizenship, and the obligations of freedom; and he loves to explore "big ideas."

His time sense is developing. He can begin to understand the sequence of past events, and he likes to relate historical events to each other. Because he is so eager to see causes and effects, he will find THE NEW BOOK OF KNOWLEDGE a source of great help.

Just as he once collected string, shells, and other objects, the junior high school pupil collects facts and information. He has intense interests. He may have several at a time, or one may follow another. Persistent interests may even fashion life careers or avocations. Do not be afraid when these multiple interests have short lives. Behind the hobbies and the changing interests, learning and maturing are going on.

In his eagerness and enthusiasm to learn many skills and extend his interests, your young adolescent may make more plans than he will ever carry out. Many plans for parties, games, and hobbies never reach completion. The planning alone satisfies the urge to be up and doing. Don't insist on a carry-through.

▶ **THE ADOLESCENT'S STANDARDS**

Just as he tries to measure his independence, just as he competes with his friends in athletics and measures his ability to get along with others, so he explores a new kind of measurement—the ethical and moral measurement of man. Your young adolescent loves to read about the heroism of great people. He thrills to the concepts of friendship and loyalty. He is interested in religious and ethical values. He loves to discuss the "right and wrong" kinds of behavior, to evaluate the ethics of a situation.

His own free reading and his junior high school curriculum reflect this interest in values. The many biographies, stories, and classics in THE NEW BOOK OF KNOWL-EDGE were selected by curriculum experts and librarians for this purpose.

▶ **HOMEWORK**

Your young adolescent will probably experience a more departmentalized school program and meet many more teachers than he did in his elementary school. Larger amounts of homework are usually assigned in grades seven, eight, and nine than in earlier grades. How, parents ask, can we help our children with home assignments? Here are some basic suggestions:

Provide proper physical conditions for studying—good light, a desk, and a comfortable chair in a quiet place.

Help your youngster establish regular study habits and times.

Provide a good dictionary and an atlas. THE NEW BOOK OF KNOWLEDGE will provide excellent reference information. Help him find other materials, too.

Create a calm home environment. Few of us can study if we are emotionally upset.

Some children need a great deal of help with homework. Some want suggestions. Others want only occasional aid in tracking down references and sources. Your interest is needed now. If homework becomes a battlefield little is accomplished.

Homework can afford an opportunity for friendly contact between parents and child. Actually, children learn more if parents do not know the answers to every question. The phrase "Let's look it up" has magic. THE NEW BOOK OF KNOWLEDGE can furnish many answers.

LANGUAGE ARTS

Language arts in grades seven, eight, and nine includes literature, grammar, spelling, and oral and written communication. Extensive reading from a variety of materials satisfies the changing interests of young adolescents.

Language arts continues to bear an important relationship to other subjects, even though your child may attend a departmentalized school. The need for expressional skills in speaking and writing, and the dependence of other subjects on reading, speaking, and listening emphasizes this relationship. Your child's language arts teacher teaches skills that are used in every other curriculum area.

REFERENCE AND RESEARCH

LITERATURE

MASS MEDIA

SOCIAL STUDIES

In grades seven, eight, and nine, social studies teaches young people about our cultural heritage and about the foundations of our democracy. Young adolescents continue to learn history, geography, economics, government, anthropology, and even some sociology, just as they did in earlier grades.

However, your junior high school youngster will now learn to "study in depth." He will learn to use a variety of instructional materials and to seek out original sources. He will be encouraged to pursue a social studies interest deeply; to look for causes, effects, and relationships; to interpret and evaluate information and sources.

THE NEW BOOK OF KNOWLEDGE provides accurate, objective, and thorough information about people, places, and events associated with every part of the globe and with every period in history. It provides your youngster with the best first source of background information to supplement his school books and to pursue an intensive study of social studies topics.

CIVIL WAR

PHYSICAL GEOGRAPHY

THE WORLD

AFRICA

AUSTRALIA AND NEW ZEALAND

ANTARCTICA

ANCIENT CIVILIZATIONS

SCIENCE

Science is an exciting subject for seventh-, eighth-, and ninth-grade pupils. Junior high school science provides stimulating exploratory experiences in biology, chemistry, physics, earth science, and other specialized courses taught in senior high school. General science is frequently a ninth-grade subject, but in many junior high schools it is taught over a period of two or three years.

The science content of THE NEW BOOK OF KNOWLEDGE reflects the latest information and the newest theories in this ever expanding field. Your junior high school youngster will find articles on such current science topics as bioluminescence; underwater exploration; lasers and masers; and quasars; as well as more familiar though no less exciting science topics.

BIOGRAPHIES OF FAMOUS SCIENTISTS

SCIENCE

MATHEMATICS

Mathematics in grades seven, eight, and nine contains many new ideas and new ways of looking at old subject matter. When your boy or girl talks about his junior high school mathematics he will use terms that may be completely unfamiliar to you. He may talk about sets and set theory; properties and structure of numbers; open and closed number sentences; commutative, associative, and distributive properties and patterns; probability; and topology.

You can help your youngster by familiarizing yourself with the meanings of these and other terms. Articles in THE NEW BOOK OF KNOWLEDGE explain the latest ideas in mathematics with clarity and simplicity. They will not only help your child to understand the new mathematics, but they will help you too.

FOREIGN LANGUAGE

Foreign language study in junior high school is both a skill and a cultural subject.

The ability to understand a foreign language has practical value in view of our country's worldwide responsibilities, and the increasing numbers of Americans who travel abroad. Foreign language study will help your child learn more about other countries and how they have contributed to our own culture.

Your child will probably begin a foreign language in grade eight or nine. However, some schools are experimenting with foreign language in the elementary grades. The study of a foreign language in the elementary and junior high schools is largely conversational.

FOREIGN LANGUAGE

Languages	L37–40
French language	F433–35; D47
French literature	F435–42, 3, 22; L128
German language	G174–81; D47
German literature	G174–81
Greek language	G349–50; A171–73
Greek literature	G350–55; D293–94; H167; A299; G356–66
Hebrew language	H100–01; C431; I 438–39
Hebrew literature	H100–03; B152–59; T15
Italian language	I 474; D47
Italian literature	I 474–81
Latin language	L76–80; K249; W238
Latin literature	L76–80
Russian language	U51
Russian literature	U51–56; F22; D298
Spanish language	S365–66; L49; D47
Spanish literature	S365–72; L70–73

HEALTH AND PHYSICAL EDUCATION

Health education is sometimes taught as part of the junior high school general science course, and sometimes as a course in hygiene. Physical education is usually conducted separately, but its contribution to the health and adjustment of young adolescents is not overlooked. Sportsmanship, teamwork, and leadership are as important as the skills that are learned.

Articles on health topics and problems that concern young people are a feature of THE NEW BOOK OF KNOWLEDGE. Your young adolescent will find reassuring articles on care of the skin, hair, eyes, and teeth; on disease, on physical fitness, and exercise; on adolescence, guidance, and mental health.

Sports and games are discussed by well-known athletes; and accurate rules, directions, and diagrams accompany the sports articles. In addition to "How to" articles on such familiar team sports as baseball, basketball, and football, experts have prepared articles on popular individual sports such as surfing, skin diving, ice-skating, golf, and many more.

HEALTH AND PHYSICAL EDUCATION

See also Health and Safety outlines for Grades K–3 and 4–6.

MUSIC

In grades seven, eight, and nine, music is usually taught by a music specialist. Your child will have many opportunities to participate in a variety of musical experiences both alone and with others. These may include part-singing in school assemblies and glee clubs, playing a musical instrument in a school orchestra or band, and taking part in musical productions.

Learning about the history of music, forms of music, and the biographies of great composers and performers is often co-ordinated with experiences in listening to recordings. The musical contributions of nations and cultures are sometimes studied as part of the social studies.

Your NEW BOOK OF KNOWLEDGE contains major articles on the history and forms of music, on musical instruments, and on the biographies of famous composers and performers. Many country articles feature special sections devoted to music.

Because teen-agers like to perform with musical groups outside of school, THE NEW BOOK OF KNOWLEDGE features articles on folk music and folk music instruments.

Dvořák, Antonin	**D366**	Mozart, Wolfgang Amadeus	**M502**
Foster, Stephen	**F389**	Offenbach, Jacques	**O55**
Franck, César	**F449**	Palestrina	**P41**
Gershwin, George	**G190**	Prokofiev, Sergei	**P477**
Gluck, Christoph Willibald	**G241**	Puccini, Giacomo	**P515**
Grieg, Edvard	**G376**	Schoenberg, Arnold	**S55**
Handel, George Frederick	**H26**	Schubert, Franz	**S58**
Handy, W. C.	**H34**	Schumann, Robert	**S59**
Haydn, Joseph	**H77**	Sibelius, Jean	**S172**
Ives, Charles	**I 487**	Strauss, Johann, Jr.	**S437**
Lind, Jenny	**L300**	Stravinsky, Igor	**S437**
Liszt, Franz	**L312**	Tchaikovsky, Peter Ilyich	**T36**
Macdowell, Edward	**M4**	Toscanini, Arturo	**T228**
Mahler, Gustav	**M30–31**	Verdi, Giuseppe	**V304**
Mendelssohn, Felix	**M219**	Wagner, Richard	**W22**

ART

Art instruction in grades seven to nine provides boys and girls with a variety of art experiences. Your child will experiment with different art media, tools, and processes. He will learn to apply art principles in his daily life at home and in the community.

Art in the seventh, eighth, and ninth grades is exploratory and experimental. Color and design are stressed because these are fundamental to all art learning. Your child will experiment with poster making, lettering, puppetry, painting, illustration, clay modeling, costume design, advertising design, and interior and stage decoration. Many schools organize after-school art clubs for boys and girls with special abilities and interests in art.

Art education provides a means of personal satisfaction for your child. Your set of THE NEW BOOK OF KNOWLEDGE offers a treasure-house of art information. There are articles presenting the history of art from prehistoric to modern times. Articles dealing with major countries of the world contain special sections devoted to art. THE NEW BOOK OF KNOWLEDGE describes art processes and art media, discusses the biographies of famous artists, and provides practical "how to" directions. THE NEW BOOK OF KNOWLEDGE is unique in its lavish use of the finest full-color art reproductions.

BIOGRAPHIES OF FAMOUS ARTISTS
AND ARCHITECTS

PRACTICAL ARTS

The practical arts in grades seven, eight, and nine include industrial arts, home economics, and typewriting.

Through industrial arts, boys and girls learn about the tools, materials, and processes of modern industry. Most schools teach woodworking. Many also teach metalwork, electrical work, mechanical drawing, printing, general crafts, and ceramics.

Home economics courses pertain to foods and food preparation, household care, home nursing, child care, dressmaking, millinery, and budgeting. In many schools, boys as well as girls study some aspects of home economics.

Typewriting instruction develops a functional skill that boys and girls will find useful in the preparation of school work and throughout their lives.

Articles in THE NEW BOOK OF KNOWLEDGE describing the practical arts were prepared by experts. These articles provide background information, and in many cases include instructions and diagrams for young people to follow.

TO PARENTS

Although THE NEW BOOK OF KNOWLEDGE is designed primarily for your elementary school child, you, too, will find it a valuable source of information.

For Pre-School Days

Even before your child is old enough to attend school, you will want to read to him from the many nursery rhymes, poems, and stories contained in THE NEW BOOK OF KNOWLEDGE. You will share with your pre-schooler the delights of looking at pictures. You will want to refer to the articles on storytelling, children's games, toys, pre-school education, and indoor activities for rainy days. You will find much to interest you in articles on health, child growth and development, psychology, family life, and baby-sitting.

For School Days

Once your child begins school you will turn to articles on learning, education, kindergarten, and schools. As your child progresses from elementary school to grades seven, eight, and nine, your NEW BOOK OF KNOWLEDGE will help you to understand your child's school curriculum. Each curriculum area is explained clearly in articles prepared by experts. The most recent trends in education and curriculum are reflected in these articles.

When your child needs help in perfecting his study skills, you can turn to articles that explain how to write a book report, how to study, or how to use reference materials. If bad weather or illness confines your child to the house, you will discover games, puzzles, and things to do or make in THE NEW BOOK OF KNOWLEDGE.

For High School Days

For the older student in your family there are many articles related to the high school curriculum. These articles are scholarly yet interesting. For science there are articles on taxonomy, genetics, vectors, and quasars; for mathematics, topology, probability, and computers; for English, the novel, the short story, and drama; for the humanities, the history of civilization, religion, art, architecture, and music.

The high school student will find practical use for the articles on colleges and universities, tests and test taking, college entrance examinations, adolescence, and vocational guidance. The topics listed below are only a sampling of the references useful to older students.

For Parents

Are you called upon to participate in a P.T.A. program? There are articles in THE NEW BOOK OF KNOWLEDGE on parent-teacher associations, ability grouping, mental health, juvenile delinquency, and driver education. Does the vocabulary of modern education puzzle you? Your NEW BOOK OF KNOWLEDGE will explain the meaning of "the new math," Initial Teaching Alphabet, and programed learning.

For the Family

When the entire family sits down to dinner there is often talk about world events, sports, entertainment, fashions, foods, or any of the hundreds of topics that families discuss. This is when THE NEW BOOK OF KNOWLEDGE rounds out its usefulness for everyone. In the Dictionary Index that concludes each volume are concise, accurate entries on thousands of additional subjects not usually included in a children's encyclopedia. How satisfying it is to be able to turn to the Dictionary Index in THE NEW BOOK OF KNOWLEDGE and find the right answer to a question quickly, easily, and at the exact moment of high interest.

HOBBIES AND LEISURE ACTIVITIES

A hobby is a favorite way of spending leisure time. Your child may share his hobby with you or with his friends; or he may follow an enthusiasm by himself.

THE NEW BOOK OF KNOWLEDGE is an especially valuable resource for pursuing a variety of hobbies. The articles listed below not only describe hobbies, but offer simple directions for each activity.

SPECIAL SKILLS

Amateur radio-operating	R62–63	Magic	M18–21
Bowling	B345–49	Moviemaking	P218–20
Guitar playing	G409–10; F329	Photography	P214–18, 201–13
Gymnastics	G428–32	Play production	P335–41
Harmonica playing	H42–43; F330	Puppetry	P534–39
		Roping	R333–35
		Ventriloquism	U301–03

A greater number of literary selections are contained in THE NEW BOOK OF KNOWLEDGE. All the selections were chosen with the advice of librarians and curriculum specialists, and are studied in schools from grades four through nine. At the same time, they are all suitable for the pure pleasure of reading at home.

The literary selections include fiction, non-fiction, and poetry; classics, short stories, legends, fairy tales, fables, myths, and rhymes. Some selections accompany the biography of a famous writer. Others appear in articles that discuss a particular type of literature. Selections suitable for younger children are listed in the K–3 section of this guide.

PROJECTS AND EXPERIMENTS

WONDER QUESTIONS

ARTICLES OF PARTICULAR INTEREST
TO PARENTS

CORRELATIONS

Below is a list of curriculum topics described in the HOME AND SCHOOL STUDY GUIDE. Each topic is correlated to articles in THE NEW BOOK OF KNOWLEDGE. These topics are arranged according to three grade levels: Kindergarten and Grades 1–3; Grades 4–6; and Grades 7–9. The grade levels are merely suggested. For additional correlations parents and teachers should also refer to related or similar topics in the other grades.

Page references in the following list refer to pages in the HOME AND SCHOOL STUDY GUIDE.